FORWARD IN Faith

THE JOURNEY FROM PURPOSE TO DESTINY

FORWARD IN *Faith*

BRENDA J STEVENSON

FORWARD in FAITH
The Journey from Purpose to Destiny
by Brenda J Stevenson
Copyright 2017
All Rights Reserved

No part of this book may be reproduced, stored in a retrieval system or transmitted in any form or by any means, electronic, mechanical, photocopying, recording or otherwise, except for the inclusion of brief quotations in a review, without prior permission in writing by the publisher.

Scripture quotations are taken from the Holy Bible, King James Version, Cambridge, 1769.

Cover Design & Interior Layout by Exodus Design Studios.

Printed in the United States of America. All rights reserved under International Copyright Law. Contents and/or cover may not be reproduced in whole or in part in any form, or by any means without written consent of the publisher.

Published by Pure Faith Publishing

ISBN 978-0692909768

For more information & resources, visit
www.forwardinfaithjourney.com

Dedication

 This book is dedicated to anyone who has ever felt like giving up on their dreams. Just know that life gets better as we continue on the journey of faith. Destiny doesn't stop here, there is yet more to do!

#keepmovingforward!

I'm on my way somewhere,
and I can't stop…won't stop,
until I get there.
….destiny

Acknowledgements

When I started this project, I didn't have a clue how it would all come together. I was simply documenting and sharing some of my struggles and how they affected my life over time. Most importantly, I wanted to be transparent and share my heart and some of the lessons that I've learned along the way. For every person who will take the time to read this book, I want you to know that even after enduring a series of disruptive storms in my life…I'm still standing! Because of those storms, I'm stronger now than I've ever been. And, to God be the glory!

I would like to thank all of my friends, near and far, for encouraging me to go all the way with this book…to believe that it was possible, and to keep writing until it was done. You know who you are. I love and appreciate each and every one of you!

To Randy, Yvonne, Britany, Earl, Angel, Nadia and Chanel: I love you to life! Thanks for loving me back.

To my mother and best friend, Mary (Babysis) Stevenson: I can't even put into words the impact your love and support has made in my life. You made the difference for me in so many ways. For sure, this book never would've been written if it weren't for your consistent encouragement, and belief in me. Thanks for making *me* believe that I could actually do it. And thanks for always being there and giving me a shoulder to cry on. For encouraging me to, "Stand, and when you feel like you can't stand…stand anyway!" I'm still standing! I love you!

To my father and Pastor, Elder Johnny W. Stevenson: You have a servant's heart, and a real love for the word of God. I have learned much from you, and I am extremely grateful. Thanks for being obedient to the calling of God on your life, and for being a great example for us to follow. I will forever be grateful for your love and support. I love you back!

Thanks to Kris, and Exodus Design Studios for a beautiful cover and layout, and for all of the additional help and support. You probably don't realize it, but you were a Godsend, and I appreciate you!

And now unto Him who is able to do exceeding, abundantly above all that I could ever ask or think. To the Sovereign God, the creator of Heaven and Earth, my source and my portion, and the One in whom I live, move and have my being. To You, I am most thankful. I'm thankful for how you've blessed and covered me over the years. Because of Your grace and mercy, and Your lovingkindness towards me, I can honestly say that I am a well-kept woman of God, and I'm eternally grateful! Thanks for being patient and not giving up on me when I was head-strong, and determined to go my own way. I've come to realize that Your way is better. In all things (past and present), Your grace is indeed sufficient. I love You!

TABLE OF *Contents*

Introduction		I
Chapter 1	It's A Process	1
Chapter 2	This Too Shall Pass	7
Chapter 3	Challenge Your Fears	11
Chapter 4	Handling Rejection	17
Chapter 5	The Truth	21
Chapter 6	Unforgiveness	29
Chapter 7	Purpose In Brokenness	37
Chapter 8	Forward After Failure	41
Chapter 9	No Guts, No Glory	49
Chapter 10	God Is A Promise Keeper	55
Chapter 11	Who I'm Becoming	63
Chapter 12	This Far By Faith	69
Poem	The Journey Forward	73
Prayer		75
Questions		77
Journal		81

Introduction

.... And the LORD said unto Moses, wherefore criest thou unto me? Speak to the children of Israel that they go forward.

Exodus 14:15

There were many times in my life when I felt like giving up on my dreams. But, somehow I knew that giving up would only make me feel worse. I knew that if I ever hoped to live a victorious life and make a mark in this world regardless of the size, I had to keep moving forward. It didn't matter what the situation or the intensity of the pain, I had to push past it and keep going. I had to find a way to live through the disappointment, the failure, the fear, and the rejection.

I discovered along the way that this was not something that I could do in my own strength. I had to learn how to lean on Jesus, surrender my will to his, and humble myself and go *through*. In the process of doing that, I had to trust that He would supply the strength, guidance and peace that I needed. Sometimes the surrender was more difficult than the situation itself, especially when I was accustomed to being in control. But, through it all, I can honestly say that his grace was and still is sufficient. I found out in the midst of many of life's gut-wrenching storms, that He is a very present help in troubling times. And, no matter how bad things get, He will never leave us nor forsake us. He is for us, and He loves us so much that He sent his only son Jesus to die for us on the cross. Therefore, the price for our sins has been paid, and now we are free to maneuver through this life operating in our gifts, sharing the love of God, and impacting lives everywhere we go for the sake of Christ.

The purpose of this book is to share some of my personal struggles and testimonies along my faith journey, and to challenge you, even as I challenge myself, to overcome every obstacle that the enemy puts in your path, and keep taking steps of faith. Be confident in the fact that our God is an intentional God, and He wants us to prosper and be in health…even as our souls prosper. My desire is to help you find encouragement in your present situation, and in whatever situation you find yourself in the future. Just know that all things are working together for your good, and that you can overcome anything that life throws at you if you just… keep …moving!

CHAPTER 1
It's a Process

    I have often heard that once you become a Christian your circle of friends gets smaller and smaller; especially if you're a *real* Christian, authentic in your faith. I'm not sure how true that is, but for whatever reason as I went through a series of challenges in my life, I looked around and found myself very much alone at 40+ years old.., discouraged, broken, and in a thousand fragmented pieces. I had been through a lot of emotional pain. In all honesty I have to admit that at that point in my life, I no longer had the desire to be around a lot of people. As I reflect back on the way things progressed, I would have to say that I believe it started with the failure of my marriage. It seems as though that was the spark that would ignite a series of perceived failures in various areas of my life, on both a personal and professional level. Maybe the self-isolation was my way of hiding from the shame of my failures and brokenness. It's one thing to fail privately when no one really knows what's going on, but to fail publicly while all of your so-called friends, family, and even worse- your enemies, are watching is just humiliating. Especially when your two biggest stumbling blocks are pride and fear…

Well, this was my life for a season. And I had to make a decision in the midst of it all as to whether I was going to lie down and die (basically give up), or pull myself up by my bootstraps, put my game face on, and make the decision to live. I chose to live. And even though I knew that the process from then on out would not be easy, I knew that someday it would all work out for my good.

Although I won't discuss them all in this book, to some, the things that I went through in my life may seem like no big deal. But they were so damaging to me that it literally affected my whole life over time. It changed who I was as a person. I wasn't a whole person anymore, but instead I became a shallow, fragmented shell of a person that was bitter, broken, and emotionally unavailable. Sadly, I failed to take the necessary steps to properly address and heal the wounds sustained in the battles. Instead, I internalized the pain and withdrew from life emotionally, socially, and eventually even physically isolating myself from people; including the ones that loved and cared about me. I put up walls so tall and fortified that when it was all said and done, no one could get in, and even scarier, I couldn't get out.

I was a prisoner in my own mind.., a prisoner of my pain, failures, disappointments, and a prisoner of fear. From the inside looking out, things sure looked grim. Isaiah 63:5 says, *"And I looked, and there was none to help; and I wondered that there was none to uphold..."* I didn't understand at the time that this was all a part of the *process*. That God was preparing me for the greater that's coming. I had not yet reached the level in my spiritual development where I fully grasped the concept of being broken for blessing. But, it was in the midst of my brokenness that I learned to humble myself and allow

God to do all that needed to be done in me…so that He could use me.

He used the brokenness of rejection to deliver me from people, and from being overly concerned with their opinions of me. He was teaching me how to stand on my own two feet, even if I had to stand alone. He wanted to remind me that I wasn't created to fit in with the crowd. He was setting me apart, and reminding me that I was in the world, but not *of* the world. He was challenging me to stand out, and have the courage to be different.

I would learn through my failures not to take myself too seriously. I was learning to trust Him more, and to lean not to my own understanding. He allowed me to know that without Him, I could do nothing; *and lest I should be exalted above measure, there is given to me a thorn in the flesh, the messenger of Satan to buffet me* (2 Corinthians 12:7).

When the enemy came to oppose me, He was teaching me that we wrestle not against flesh and blood, but against principalities, against powers, against rulers of the darkness of this world, against spiritual wickedness in high places (Ephesians 6:12).

Through my seasons of brokenness, He taught me that in order to fight spiritual battles, I would have to learn how to employ my spiritual muscles, and to have them strengthened by reason of use (Hebrews 5:14). This consisted of having an active prayer life and frequently meditating on his word. It meant putting on the whole armor of God. In the midst of the isolation, the loneliness, and the silence…God had my full attention.

I began the process of surrendering my will to His, and

allowing him to do the work in me so that I could be better. With his help and guidance I began to tear down walls... brick by brick and layer after layer until I got to what I believe was the core of the problem. Do you know what I discovered? I discovered that the problem was me...

First of all, who wants to admit to themselves that at the very center of all that is going totally and completely wrong in life is me, myself and I...and these three are one! YOU! Leading the way, calling the shots and wreaking havoc in your own life at every turn. No one is safe. In your mind, if there's a problem...it's the other person's fault. If we don't click with someone, then they just don't like us for no apparent reason. Now, I realize that there are always going to be some haters out there, and people who will try to dim your light in order to make theirs shine brighter. Unfortunately, this is frequently the case with women. It's true that we as women are more often than not, very hard on each other. We appear to be very competitive within our gender. And instead of supporting and lifting each other up, we have a tendency to tear one another down. It's shameful, honestly, and I wish it weren't so. Nevertheless, we can't be the victim in *every* situation. At some point we have to take a step back, do some self-reflection, and deal with the real issues that are deeply rooted inside of us, and buried beneath layers of pain, disappointment and dysfunction.

If we can get free in our minds from the negative self image and thoughts that the enemy has downloaded, we could have the whole world literally at our finger tips. There would be no limit to what we could do. We could live out all of the things that we even dare to dream of if we could just...get...free.

Truthfully, I lived in bondage for years because it took me a while to get it…to really get it. Some lessons had to be taught over and over again because when testing time came I was still failing. I was still struggling in my flesh and wrapped up in pride, and as the scripture tells us, *pride goes before destruction and a haughty spirit before a fall* (Proverbs 16:18).

God was teaching me that humility comes before honor. That I would have to endure some things in order to shape and strengthen my character. He assured me that the trials would not kill me, but it would be painful and I would be stretched. I had to be stretched so that I could reach and fit into my position…my next level.

When God wants to do something amazing in your life, He has to be sure that when he puts you out there to represent Him before the world that you will be able to handle the blessing. He has to be sure that you won't abuse the power that comes with the position. And that your character and integrity will hold up under the pressure so that when people start to praise and speak well of you, you won't get caught up in the hype and start believing your own press. He wants us to stay humble, rooted and grounded in the word of God so that we don't lose sight of our purpose.

When we find ourselves going through the hard places in life, the place of struggle, brokenness, isolation, and testing; He wants us to remember that it's all part of the process. At the end of the day, we have to realize that we don't come to the place of brokenness, pain, isolation and struggle to stay there. The point is to go *through*. And, in the midst of going through, He wants us to remember where our help comes from, and to acknowledge that He is our source. It's in Him that we live, move, and have our being (Acts 17:28).

CHAPTER 2
This Too, Shall Pass

I don't know about you, but I've learned to appreciate seasons because seasons change. I've come to understand that life is a constant cycle of trials and tribulations, successes and failures, ups and downs, good times and bad. The blessing in it is realizing that whatever we are facing at any given time in our lives, it's only for a season. God will never allow us to suffer any trial beyond what we are able to bear.

The late Reverend James Cleveland used to sing a song that I still love today called, "*This Too Shall Pass.*" The message of the song is basically that whatever you're going through, no matter what it is, it didn't come to stay; it came to *pass*. Trouble doesn't last always. Eventually, the storm has got to pass over. This too shall pass! At the same time, there's a certain level of maturity that comes with accepting the fact that many of the good things that we enjoy have an end as well. That just means that we have outgrown where we are, and the end to that season of success is motivation for us to move on to bigger and better things. We are too comfortable and have become stagnant or complacent. But it's only unfortunate for those who don't want to go higher.

The goal is to keep moving forward on the path that God has set before us because eyes have not seen, ears have not heard, and neither has entered into the hearts of men what God has prepared for those that love Him (1 Corinthians 2:9). Life simply cannot be all good without anything to test our faith in God. If it were, we wouldn't need God, and we certainly wouldn't be striving to make it to Heaven. Heaven would be right here on Earth. Every day can't be sunshine. There is going to be some rain. But, we can't neglect to give God praise even in the rainy seasons of our lives because it's the rain that causes things to grow. The seasons of life help us to grow and learn and become better, more well-balanced people every day. Seasons teach us lessons and open up windows and opportunities for blessing every time we advance to another level. I am thankful for a God who knows exactly what it takes to get me where I need to be. The very God who created me, and before I was even formed in the womb, He knew me (Jeremiah 1:5). He knows my end from my beginning, and He sees me as I will be, the finished product.., fearfully and wonderfully made.

Regardless of the trial you're facing or the heartbreak or brokenness you're experiencing, just remember that this too shall pass. Life doesn't stop and stand still. Time keeps moving and our job is to keep moving right along with it. Roll with the punches. Don't get stuck and stay where you are. Keep moving forward, one step and one day at a time. We all know that setbacks can slow us down. That's ok; we're human. At times it may be necessary to take a minute to catch your breath and regroup. Move slowly if you have to, crawl if you must…but just keep moving. You can't stop because destiny doesn't stop here. There is yet more to do.

God has an awesome plan and purpose for your life, and you have an obligation.., a responsibility to see it through. Why do you think you are still here, walking the earth? You have a divine assignment, a destiny, and dreams to fulfill.., and it's all inside of you waiting for the right time and season to be birthed out. It's normal to be nervous about it, and even unsure as to what your purpose and assignment is. But, the only way to discover it is to keep moving.

Get into the presence of God and keep dreaming, keep discovering new and wonderful things about yourself, your gifts, talents and abilities. Get into His presence and discover *who* He created you to be, and *all* He created you to be. And use your gifts, talents and abilities to bless the world for His glory.

CHAPTER 3
Challenge Your Fears

Many of my friends and family would be surprised to learn that I know what it's like to be insecure and have low self-esteem. I know what it's like to want to fit in, but don't, want to be confident, but you're not. I know what it's like to seemingly fear everything…including myself. To fear that I may potentially fail at something that I really want to do, but even more than that.., to fear my potential to one day do or be something greater than I ever thought possible.

Fear is an emotion that touches every life at some point in time. In Christendom, we call fear a *spirit.* It's something that we either face and conquer, or run from and allow it to conquer us. We do this time and time again until we eventually give up and resolve to sit on the sidelines and watch other people live out their dreams. Tell me, at what point do you decide to rise up, take a stand and begin to go after your destiny with all of the energy, drive, and passion that God intended? I'm willing to go out on a limb and suggest that *now* is the time, and *this* is the point in your life when you make the decision to step out in faith. To decide in your heart, that you are moving forward, in spite of your current circumstances.

In the book of Exodus, when Moses was leading the children of Israel out of the bondage and captivity of Egypt, they were fearful because Pharaoh and his army were pursuing them. They started to believe that they were better off staying in Egypt because they feared dying in the wilderness. They didn't have the faith to believe that God would protect them.

In the midst of their crying and complaining, Moses encouraged them and told them not to be afraid. He told them to stand still and watch what the Lord was about to do on their behalf. He went on to say, "The Egyptians you see today, you shall see them no more forever." He assured them that God was going to destroy their enemies, and all they had to do was keep moving forward (Exodus 14:13-15).

The same message applies to us today. God doesn't want us to worry about our enemies or the failures of our past. He's letting us know that He will fight every battle for us. All we have to do is hold our peace and focus on moving forward. He will instruct us and make a way for us as we go (Exodus 14:16).

The older I get, the more I realize that I would rather face my fears and fail, than to risk the regret of never having at least taken a chance at doing something great. To do something so far outside of my comfort zone that I would need the strength, grace, and wisdom of God to get me through it. Never in a million years did I think that I would actually write and publish a book, but there were seasons in my life when I felt led to journal. My most vivid memories of those seasons occurred while I was stationed in Okinawa, Japan. I remember spending the majority of my weekends at the beach on the Army base at Torii Station during the spring and summer months of 2008 and 2009. I would start the day off sitting by the water journaling, and having my quiet time with God. My journaling consisted mostly of spiritual thoughts and things that I sensed the Lord was saying to me…or even things that I felt like saying to myself.

Journaling has always been a great way to help me process and deal with my pain. Those quiet times alone on the beach were therapy for me in a lot of ways. It was during those times that I recall feeling the most at peace. I started sensing that God was doing something more in me. I sensed that He was about to challenge me to take a leap of faith and get out of the boat where I felt comfortable *and safe..*, and risk being uncomfortable and vulnerable. As I continued to pray, read my bible and put my thoughts on paper, over time I started to see the beginnings of a book come into form; and the image of a dream being birthed in my heart. At first, I only jokingly entertained it, but then, all of a sudden I started asking myself, "Why not?"

That's what we all should be asking ourselves when it comes to making the decision to pursue our dreams. At the end of the day, the worst thing that can happen is that it just doesn't work out. And, so what if it doesn't? At least you *tried* it. So now, either you have the passion and drive to keep trying until you achieve the success you desire, or you count your losses and move on to something that you are better suited for. Find and follow your passion, and let God be your guide. "Trust in the Lord with all of your heart and lean not to your own understanding. In all thy ways acknowledge Him, and He will direct your path." (Proverbs 3:5).

I've always enjoyed writing because I feel like I express myself well through my written words. But, writing a book is on a whole different level. I never really knew how or where to start or even what to say. But I continued to seek the Lord's guidance and direction, and He was faithful to bring me through to completion.

Regardless of the lies the enemy has tricked us into believing about ourselves, we are good enough. We are enough, period! We have within us everything it takes to be successful, but we have to be courageous enough to give ourselves permission to try, and then commit to the process. It can be done; and it can be done by you if you have the faith to believe God for it. I can only imagine what amazing things God could, and would, do for us if we would only dare to step out in faith and try. As I stated before, time waits for no one. It keeps rolling right along. We might as well roll with it or get left behind. It takes faith to take risks, but God responds to faith.

Just like the people in the bible parable that the rich man gave the talents to. The ones who were courageous enough to take risks and invest those talents received increase, while the one who was afraid and hid his talent not only failed to gain anything, but he also lost what he had (Matthew 25:14-30).

Take a chance at something. Endeavor to discover the possibilities right at your fingertips. We were created to be creative...to do something great in this life, to fulfill our life's purpose and reach our destiny. And God wants to see us try...

When we move forward in faith in spite of our fears and

anxieties, that's another opportunity to overcome and frustrate the enemy. It doesn't matter how small the step is, just take that next step. Small victories are victories, nonetheless! Don't quit. Never give up. Go all the way! Move forward and experience the power of freedom in the presence of fear, *for where the Spirit of the Lord is, there is liberty* (2 Corinthians 3:17).

CHAPTER 4
Handling Rejection

Another thing that many of us have, and still do struggle with is rejection. What I can tell you from first-hand experience is that this is a *very strong spirit*. Rejection was a mighty stronghold in my life for a very long time. As I mentioned in the previous chapter, it was the result of many offenses and painful experiences that went unaddressed for years. Instead of finding a way to deal with my pain and address my issues, I handled it the only way I knew how at the time, and did my best to go on with my life.

Again, I suspect that the root of my struggle with rejection goes back to the breaking down of my marriage, and subsequent divorce. From there, it just started to grow and take on a life of its own. I didn't understand at the time that the rejection was a weapon that the enemy had formed against me to keep me from my destiny. It worked for a while, as I proceeded to internalize my pain, dress my wounds, and build up walls all around me so that I couldn't be hurt anymore. No one could get close enough to me to hurt or disappoint me, and if they did manage to disappoint, it didn't matter much because I wasn't expecting much from them anyway. Well, the problem with that is.., if you refuse to let anyone get close to you, you become a very cold, callous and untrusting person who cannot be effectively used by God because you have become emotionally unavailable. No one can get close enough to you to experience the gift of God that *is* you.

I became so numb in the process of doing this that I was unable to feel anything much, emotionally. The lies of the enemy affected every area of my life, and almost literally shut me down. It seemed like I had become such an empty shell to the point where people could feel the insincerity in me when I tried to show or act like I was concerned about them. When I made a genuinely sincere attempt at it, it was for me an empty emotion, and it showed. Don't get me wrong, I wanted to show genuine concern. I wanted to *feel* genuine concern. I just couldn't. Believe me when I tell you that people know what's real and what's not. They can sense insincerity in us like predators can sense weakness and fear in their potential prey. On the other hand, real love can be felt because real love has everything to do with God. He is love in its true form, which means that it can be felt and experienced, and it can change and save lives.

The spirit of rejection can cause us to isolate ourselves and live a life of loneliness and defeat, and that just simply is not the will of God for our lives. God wants us to be free and live life abundantly. Not just financially. Not even primarily financially, but abundant in love, joy, peace, long suffering, gentleness, goodness, faith, meekness and temperance (Galatians 5:22-23).

If we give in to the spirit of rejection, the enemy of our soul wins, period, end of story. We should never allow him to win because the bible teaches us that he is already defeated. But at the same time, we can't just sit back and think that God is going to do all of the work. We have to fight to be delivered and set free. God has given us everything we need to be victorious through His word. Luke 10:19 shows us the authority we have over the enemy: *Behold, I give you power to tread on serpents and scorpions, and power over all the power of the enemy and nothing shall by any means harm you.*

We should be ready to give and receive love freely. The bible tells us that love covers a multitude of sins, and that there is no fear in love. Fear has torment, and God has not given us the spirit of fear, but of love, power and a sound mind (2 Timothy 1:7). Again, we see where God has given us power through His holy word. Just reading the scriptures should give us renewed confidence daily because it gives us knowledge of the spiritual authority we have in the name of Jesus. If we are not free to receive love and be delivered from the stronghold of rejection that has us tied up and emotionally bankrupt; then we don't have the capacity to give love freely to anyone else, no matter how much we want to. You can't give to others what you don't possess. Charity begins at home, and in this case that means you. Love yourself first! Minister to yourself, and your spiritual and emotional needs first by spending time in the presence of the Lord so that you can get the rest, peace, and healing renewal that your soul so desperately needs. Start in prayer, in your quiet time with God so that you can begin to tear down every prison wall that the enemy helped you build around your life. Brick by fortified brick, lie after life-shattering lie. Tear down those walls! Fight to get free so that you can live not just the rest of your life, but the *best* of your life, in Christ Jesus!

Don't be deceived, though. Fear, rejection, and fear *of* rejection are not easy spirits to overcome. I have struggled with them for years. I believe that the only thing that gave me the courage to keep moving was the fact that I had strong roots in my faith and my walk with God. Honestly, it's an ongoing battle, but I'm still in the fight. I haven't given up, and I'm taking steps of faith toward my future and destiny. This book is proof. So, let me encourage you today, to begin to speak life over yourself and your dreams…whatever they are. Just know that *all things are possible to them that believe* (Mark 9:23). Begin in faith to aggressively pursue deliverance through continual prayer and the truth of the Word of God, and be set free, in Jesus name!

CHAPTER 5
The Truth

At some point in time, I'm sure we have all heard and likely used the scriptural saying, *"The truth shall set you free."* Although it was quoted mostly in the context of a joke, the fact of the matter is that this is a very powerful piece of scripture. Out of all of the *Aha!* moments I've had in the past, this one is probably the most profound. Let me tell you why.

Many of us go through life oblivious to the truth of what God's word says about being free. We stay in bondage because we simply don't know (or actively believe) the truth. It seems a lot easier to believe a lie from the enemy rather than believe (and receive) the truth of God's word. We have all been guilty of it in the past, and many of us still struggle with it now. We walk around in shackles and chains in a self-imposed prison because the enemy of our minds has convinced us to walk in fear, failure and low self-esteem. But, if we could ever get up the courage to challenge the enemy and begin to speak the truth of God's word over our situation, our lives would change for the better, and we would grow exponentially!

I'll share a personal example of how the enemy deceived

me into believing a lie that had a far-reaching and very damaging effect in many areas of my life. I was in the process of retiring when I was diagnosed with Social Anxiety Disorder. This is a common condition that is very similar to and often confused with extreme shyness. Not everybody's symptoms are the same. It affects people in many different ways. My struggles mostly consisted of avoiding small talk, dreading being the center of attention, public speaking, and fear of the possibility of being judged and/or rejected by others.

The truth of the matter is that many people struggle with various forms of anxiety, but for the most part have learned to manage it well enough to function in their daily lives. I would humorously call it being *functionally anxious*. It may not seem like a big deal on the surface, but if it is allowed to get out of control, it can negatively affect your personal and professional relationships, and stop you from enjoying a full and meaningful life.

I was quick to accept the diagnosis because I was dealing with a lot of emotional pain, and I did appear to be struggling in this area. The only people I was comfortable with were those that I knew genuinely cared about me unconditionally. And in my mind, that was not a very long list. I had completely lost sight of the concept of just being myself and allowing things to flow naturally. I was so nervous and anxious in certain situations that I would do everything in my power to avoid interacting with people around me because I felt socially awkward. I wasn't comfortable engaging in normal every day conversation; especially with people that I didn't know, or feel like I had anything in common with. This was a stark contradiction to how I used to be during the early and mid years of my military career. I was very sociable, outgoing, and really enjoyed being around people. I had even outgrown the shyness that I carried all the way through high school. It was truly astonishing years later to look at my reflection in the mirror and see a person that I no longer recognized staring back at me.

Sure, I knew how to put my game face on (my mask), to make it through the day. Especially while still on active duty. I could function on the job because I had to. I had no choice but to try to cope and keep going. Some days were better than others. And then there were days that I just failed miserably! Of course, no one really noticed those off days but me because they didn't really know me well enough to detect the change in me. But, I knew me.., and I remembered the strong, confident, outgoing person that I used to be...and this clearly was not her.

Obviously, these issues didn't take over my life overnight. Instead it was a slow, gradual process of internalizing the pain of perceived rejection, disappointments, and the failures of my past.

Notice though, that I said *perceived* rejection. I say that because a lot of what we think is rejection from others really isn't. Nine times out of ten, most people aren't even judging or forming an opinion of us either way. But, because we have now been programmed to process and over analyze everything in a negative light as directed by the enemy, we automatically assume the worst. That's what we do. We close the book before we even finish the story; whereas…if we would take the time to relax, breathe, and give people a chance, we would likely discover that *there be more for us than against us* (2 Kings 6:16).

But, to the contrary, my internal system was set to self-destruct as soon as I found myself in an uncomfortable social situation. Most times, without fail I would crash and burn. Not in a big way, but subtly. It was probably no big deal to them. They probably just assumed I was awkward, stand-offish or stuck-up, and would eventually move on...or I would. For me, this was extremely stressful and discouraging, and it seemed like a hopeless situation. I viewed it as a personal failure, and I began to withdraw, self-isolate and go into hiding.

Because the people who were close to me didn't know or understand what I was going through, they didn't know how to take me. Even some of the people I loved and cared about and knew they felt the same about me, found my behavior stand-offish and aloof. And you know how quickly women can judge each other with the whole, *she thinks she's better than everybody* conversation. Oh, I'm more than sure that happened on many occasions...and I get it. I'm sure I would've felt the same way even if I didn't verbalize it. But little did they know that I was deeply wounded and fragile...literally a thousand pieces of brokenness...and I was hanging on by a thread. Desperately trying to survive and function to the best of my limited ability. Willing myself to find the strength to smile when all I wanted to do was cry. Forcing myself to laugh when in my life, nothing was funny...

When you're hurting inside and you don't know where to turn, who can you talk to...especially when you can't even find the words to articulate it, or put it into sentences? Who would even understand unless they've been through or experienced similar pain?

We have a tendency to think that talking to family (or seeking professional help, if that is your preference), is the answer to dealing with all of our emotional woes, but I would beg to differ. Not always. My parents are great. They have always been a strong support system for me, and that has never failed. I thank God for them, and I love them dearly. But, the truth of the matter in painful situations like this is that all they can do is love you through the pain. No matter how hard they try, or how much they wish they could.., they can neither fix it nor take the pain away. You literally have no other choice…if you're a fighter…than to walk-that-thing-out! Put one foot in front of the other and keep moving forward. It's a process, but there is purpose in the pain. For those of us who are spiritual and believe God to bring us through every situation, we know that the quicker we submit to God and allow Him to do the work in us, the quicker and more effectively healing will come (Philippians 1:6).

I was saved during this season of my life, but still somewhat struggling in my understanding. I had seen God do some amazing things but yet, I didn't know I had spiritual authority over this thing that was weighing me down and affecting literally every-area-of-my-life! The constant failure and daily battle was both, physically and emotionally draining…but God!

In the real world, you can't just decide to stay home from work because you are struggling in your personal life. Not only did I have to go but, I had to perform. I had to be the leader that I had worked so hard to become as a Chief while feeling like a failure myself. I had to find a way to offer encouragement to others when I needed it myself. I had to help find resolution for other peoples' issues but, had no clue how to overcome my own. But, God gave me what I needed on a daily basis. He gave me just enough grace to deal with the issues of that day, and brand new mercies every morning. Great was His faithfulness towards me, and His strength made perfect in my weakness.

God sustained me, and gave me the strength to function effectively at my job for the remainder of my time in service. I was just entering my second year in Okinawa, Japan when I made the decision to end my military career. I was tired, damaged, and in desperate need of healing and restoration. It really didn't take much deliberation. I immediately felt at peace, and viewed it as a sign of God's approval. I believe He was letting me know that I had made the right decision. *Come unto me all ye that labour and are heavy laden, and I will give you rest* (Matthew 11:28).

I had gone as far as I would go in that chapter of my life. It was time to move on to the next one which would begin with me taking the time to heal and start the process of becoming a whole person again. It was going to be a tedious process, but I was in it to win it! This was God's doing, and I knew within myself that it was a necessary work.

If I ever hoped to be a vessel greatly used by God, I could not continue to be the empty shell of a person who was emotionally unavailable and detached from the world around me. I would have to be set free in my mind, which meant that I had to know and connect with the truth of God's word on a whole different level. I had to move beyond surface level worship and really connect with the fact that Jesus bled, suffered, and went all the way to Calvary to die for the remission of my sins.

I had to know beyond a shadow of a doubt that He died so that I could live…free. Because of the blood of Jesus, the enemy of my soul can no longer just come and attack and destroy my life without permission from God. Basically, he's got to go through Jesus in order to get to me! Yep, those are the rules. And the enemy has no choice *but* to abide by them.

Well, I don't know how you feel about it, but making the decision to explore and understand that truth on a higher level changed my life! It assures me that every trial, every storm or negative situation that touches my life has already been approved by God. He allowed it because it's going to serve a purpose in my life. It's going to make me better, stronger, and more effective. Our God is sovereign, and even though we can't always see it, we know that He is behind the scenes and beneath the surface working *all things* together for our good…in every situation (Romans 8:28).

Just knowing and really believing these truths helps me to trust God more and more every day, and live a more confident life. Not in my own strength, but in the strength of the One who created me, and gave His life for me.

In times of adversity, it is not God's will that we shrink back in fear, get stuck and stay where we are. It is always His will that we keep taking steps of faith. I'm reminded, even in this moment to be joyful in spite of what lies ahead of me because *the joy of the Lord is my strength* (Nehemiah 8:10), and He will keep them in perfect peace whose mind is stayed on Him (Isaiah 26:3).

No matter what comes against you.., keep praying, keep

loving, keep forgiving, keep helping, keep believing, keep creating, keep living, keep smiling, keep hope alive! ...And *keep moving forward!*

CHAPTER 6
Unforgiveness

Before moving any further in this book, I think it's important to touch on the subject of unforgiveness and the negative effect it has on our ability to move forward. Unforgiveness is usually the result of perceived offenses that we have suffered at the hand of another person or persons. The free dictionary defines an offense as the act of causing anger, resentment, displeasure or affront. It is further defined online as an annoyance or resentment brought about by a perceived insult or disregard for oneself or one's standards or principles.

In the book of Luke, Jesus tells us in a matter-of-fact kind of way that offenses will come, and that no one is exempt. He says that, *"it is impossible that no offenses should come, but woe to him through whom they come!"* (Luke 17:1). But, He goes on to say how we are to forgive regardless of the frequency of the offense, *"Take heed to yourselves: If thy brother trespass against thee, rebuke him; and if he repent, forgive him. And if he trespass against thee seven times in a day, and seven times in a day turn again to thee, saying, I repent; thou shalt forgive him."* (Luke 17:3-4).

Many times, the single most predominant thing that gets us off track and prevents us from moving forward in life is bitterness and resentment, which are both rooted in unforgiveness. When we have been hurt or wronged by someone, especially someone we trust, we have a tendency to hold on to that hurt because we believe that it holds them hostage to us for the pain that they have caused. In our minds, our failure to forgive them in some way keeps them from living a happy and productive life. Nothing could be further from the truth. I can almost guarantee you that the person who mistreated or harmed you has moved on. More than likely, the only person that's still stuck in that moment is you. The only person still miserable and unhappy is you.

Unforgiveness is a heavy weight to carry around. It clouds our judgment and prevents us from living our best life. We become a stumbling block to ourselves when we refuse to let go of an offense. It's like adding insult to injury, and becoming our own worst enemy when we continue to replay the hurt over and over again in our mind. Truthfully, we're doing far more damage than good, and literally forfeiting our God-given power to control our own destiny.

Harboring offenses in our heart keeps our heart from being truly healed, and keeps us from being fully free. Forgiveness, as the saying goes, is a gift that we give ourselves. It frees us from the bondage of hurt, pain, and dysfunction that stifles us and fills us with all kinds of toxic emotions. While it doesn't absolve the person who hurt us of the injustice they did to us; it empowers us to let go of the past and begin to chart the path to our future and a healthy, joyful, and productive life.

I remember a time several years ago when I was struggling with unforgiveness in my heart. It came at a time when I was making great progress in my healing process, and God was restoring me and helping me put the broken pieces of my life back together. And then, right in the middle of making progress, I experienced a setback through an offense by a person whom I considered like family. To me, the offense was an act of betrayal, and it hit me hard. And even though I was quick to end the friendship and sever the ties, just like in times past, I still internalized the pain of it, and kept the offense in the back of my mind instead of dealing with it head on. And it started manifesting itself in ways I didn't even understand.

That offense opened the door to unforgiveness, and *boom!* There it was…the enemy's way in through a door that I had left wide open for him, and he took full advantage of the opportunity. Before I even knew what hit me, I was walking around with a dark cloud over my head, and one in my heart. It was a spirit of bitterness, and probably depression, and it was heavy! I went from being on cloud nine and on top of the world; to storm clouds and now the world is on top of me. My relationships were affected and how I dealt with people in general was altered. I didn't trust anyone, and I didn't want to be around anyone…not even my family.

I tried wholeheartedly to pray because I knew that it was affecting me, and not in a good way. The problem was, I had opened myself up to trust again, and once again, I was let down. It seemed to me like I was always considerate of the feelings of others, but no one seemed to have any regard for mine. I was tired…extremely tired of being disappointed by the people that I cared about. And with this last betrayal, it seemed like something in me just broke. I kept replaying the betrayal over and over in my mind. I just couldn't seem to let it go. Its hold on me was so strong and firm that it felt like it had a grip on my soul. In hindsight, I have to wonder if I wasn't just holding onto it so that I would have a reason to feel sorry for myself because dysfunction had become my normal.

One morning I was asleep on the couch in my living room because I had an event that weekend. I had guest staying overnight and every room was filled. This event had been planned for months, so although I was hard pressed to cancel it, I decided against it. While I was sleeping, I had a dream which consisted of about three different segments. In the dream, someone was trying to kill me. In the first segment, I was at the gas station pumping gas into my tank when a strange man walked right up to me with a gun and pulled the trigger at point blank range—boom! Fade to black. The next segment was almost the same except I was in the car and had someone with me, but I was never clear on whom that was. Anyway, the same strange man walked up to my side of the car window, aimed the gun directly at me at point blank range, and pulled the trigger...fade to black.

The same scenario, like a short film on rewind happened one last time—same man, same gun, pulled the trigger at point blank range...fade to black. Each time he walked up to me in the dream I remember thinking as he pointed the gun at me, *Oh God.., he's going to kill me!* And then he would pull the trigger. Now, I never actually saw myself die. Perhaps that's a good thing. It always faded to black immediately after the gunfire. But here is where it gets good.

Right at the end of the last segment of the dream when the gunman had pulled the trigger the third and final time, I woke up to Bishop TD Jakes preaching on one of the gospel stations. It was about seven o'clock on a Sunday morning, and right at that moment he was saying, "The enemy has released a murdering spirit over your life, and he means to destroy you—I mean literally take—you—out!" What are the odds that I would wake up right at *that* moment from *that* dream to hear the man of God speaking *that* word of knowledge?

Well, if you think about it, I would say it's pretty clear that anyone who is trying to kill you is an enemy. And if they are aiming a gun at you at point blank range, make no mistake about it- they mean to utterly destroy you! I felt like it was God's way of letting me know in no uncertain terms, that the enemy was trying to use that betrayal and all of the pain of my past to make me bitter, resentful, depressed and untrusting all over again.., especially now that I was making so much progress in my healing. The goal was to make me shut down and go back to the old habits of self-isolating, and believing that my life had no value, and that no one really cared about me. But instead, God showed me the truth. He showed me that I must be a force to be reckoned with in my future. I must be a mighty weapon in the hands of God. That *MUST* be what the enemy knows about me that I don't yet know about myself. Otherwise, he wouldn't fight me so hard. I mean, nobody puts a contract out on a person whom they don't feel threatened by in some way…right? You better know it!

God wanted me to know the truth so that the truth would set me free. He wanted me to know what I was dealing with. And, that I had the power to overcome…to resist the enemy and take back everything that he had stolen from me. I understood that it had to begin with my willingness to release the debt of the offense that I was harboring against my friend (and anybody else for that matter), *and forgive*. We learn in Matthew 6:14-15, that forgiveness is a requirement. If we fail to forgive others for their wrongs against us, then neither will our Heavenly Father forgive us for our wrongs.

Trust me; He knows what we are going through at all times. He knows the wrongs we have been dealt, and the mistreatment and injustices we have suffered at the hands of others. But He says, "Vengeance is mine; I will repay." (Romans 12:19). We don't have to fight our own battles. And we shouldn't be walking around with a chip on our shoulder full of bitterness and resentment towards others. We're blocking our own blessings- not anyone else's! Let go of that stuff, and live-your-life!

That personal encounter with God blew my mind. He knew that I was hurting and needed to be delivered. I was going down fast and felt I had nowhere to turn because again, who would understand something that I couldn't even explain myself?

Well listen, when I tell you that immediately I was set free, that is no exaggeration. It was instant deliverance. The blessing for me was in knowing that God took that moment to personally minister deliverance to his daughter whom He loves passionately and unconditionally, in spite of her flaws and shortcomings. He saw me struggling and carrying the weight of something that was too heavy for me, and He set me free. Just like that! He knows the healing power that our willingness to forgive brings, and He knows exactly what it will take to bring us through to victory. Suddenly, everything changed. The dark clouds lifted, there was genuine joy in my laughter, and I felt as light as a feather.

That experience changed the way that I see things spiritually. I've learned to look beyond surface, and try to focus on my faith, and what I've learned through my experiences. It is not a perfect world that we live in. Offenses are going to come, period. We barely find the strength to get past one offense before we are almost immediately faced with another. But, we have the power to choose how we respond to each and every one of them; whether we stay stuck in it, or whether we choose to forgive and move forward on our path to destiny.

It's important to know that without the strength of the Lord, we can do nothing; least of all fight spiritual battles. We simply cannot win if we do not seek the Lord's strength and guidance, and both come from being in His presence. If we commit to making the Lord our priority by spending quiet moments with Him in worship, prayer, and reading his Word, joy is one of the many fruit of the Spirit that our Father will grace us with.

I have had many battles with depression over the years, as I'm sure some of you have; even as a Christian. It was so heavy at times that I could barely lift myself up because of the weight of it. Depression is like a dark, gloomy cloud hovering over your life, and it has to be dealt with swiftly before the enemy can get a serious stronghold on you. Pray! And press your way through. Cut it off at the pass.

Like I mentioned before, we have to *know* that we have that authority, in Jesus name (Luke 10:19). Our Savior, the Lord, Jesus Christ is alive and well, and through His Word, He is still winning battles and saving souls today. *Heaven and earth shall pass away, but the word of God shall stand forever* (Matthew 24:35).

Now, please understand that the authority spoken of in Luke 10:19 isn't just given to us arbitrarily. That kind of power comes through relationship with God. Otherwise, we find ourselves in a, *"Jesus I know, and Paul I know, but who are you?"* kind of predicament (Acts 19:15). *"Ain't nobody got time for that!"*

It means knowing His voice and being obedient to His perfect will for our lives, and making every effort to do what He has called us to do. We can't overcome the attacks of the enemy in our own strength, but His strength is made perfect in our weakness. God will give us victory over the enemy and every trap that he sets to try to destroy us, but we must do our due diligence to pray and meditate on the Word of God, and activate it in our lives.

CHAPTER 7
Purpose in Brokenness

My philosophy on life stems from the belief that nothing just happens. Everything that God allows to occur in our lives is for a reason. It doesn't matter whether it's a good or bad thing, or a big or small thing; it all has its purpose for existing in our lives. I think it's fair to say that most of us have had our fair share of brokenness. I'm even more confident we would agree that brokenness is painful. Anytime something in the human body is broken, there is pain associated with that brokenness. A broken arm causes pain, a broken leg, a broken hand…and even a broken heart.

Whatever the broken part is, the pain it causes gets our attention. The first thing we generally do is go to the doctor so that he can address the injured or ailing part, get to the source of that pain and give you a treatment plan to put you on the path to healing. Healing is a process; it takes time. Underneath the cast of a broken limb healing is taking place, even though you can't see it or feel it. And so it is with our spiritual brokenness. Even though we can't always see it, beneath the surface healing is taking place and God is the doctor who addresses the source of our pain, treats it, and brings healing to our situation…if we let Him.

God speaks to us through our pain because it is then that He has our full attention (Psalm 51:17). What we are going through at that moment in time may not feel good at all; in fact, it may seem unbearable, but our sincere brokenness and humility brings us closer to God. He knows he can use us in our broken state because it's in those times that we begin to let go of pride and all of those outside interferences that keep us from hearing him, and being open to what he is trying to do in us and through us. His ways are past finding out, but I do know that what the devil meant for evil, God will turn it around and make it good (Genesis 50:20).

God often allows us to experience pain and brokenness as a consequence of our own actions, and unfortunately, sometimes through no fault of our own. Sometimes bad things happen to good people. But if you've lived long enough to have gone through some things, then I'm sure you know by now that it's all a part of life. We have to take the good with the bad. The blessing is in how we choose to respond to it. In fact, one of the most important lessons I have ever had to learn is how to keep the right attitude and perspective in the midst of my storms, and *choosing* to respond to them in a positive way.

In essence, it's not *what* you go through that should be the primary focus but, *how* you go through it. It takes faith… but don't worry; God will give you many opportunities to get it right. It is so vitally important that we learn from our experiences so that we don't continue to make the same mistakes and bad choices in life. If you are not paying attention to what God is doing, you'll miss it and delay the healing process. Or even worse, you may cause the injured part (you) to have to be broken again, and reset in order to restart the process so that total healing and restoration can take place.

No matter what you are going through, I want you to know today that God has your back, and He wants to bring healing to your situation right now (Psalm 34:18). The Potter wants to rebuild and restore your broken places. He wants to mold you and shape you, and do a mighty work in your life. Although weeping may endure for a night, take comfort in knowing that joy is right around the corner. All you have to do is turn the page. Get up from where you are and take another step forward. Keep living, keep breathing, and keep believing!

Believe that joy is possible…even in your current situation. Believe that healing and restoration are possible…even when the pain is still fresh. Believe in the power of the blood of Jesus, and know that all things are possible to them that *believe!*

CHAPTER 8
Forward After Failure

 Everybody goes through something in life that qualifies as failure. It doesn't matter who you are, where you come from, your race, age, gender, ethnicity, social status, or any other demographic. You will, if you haven't already, experience failure on some level. Although it may be unfortunate, it doesn't define who you are. It just proves that no one is exempt from hard times, and that you're human like the rest of us. It doesn't matter whether you choose to play it safe and stay in your comfort zone, or if you're the type that's willing to take some risks. Eventually, failure in one form or another will find itself parked on your street.

 My first major experience with failure was divorce. The failure of divorce is a blow that has the potential to knock the wind out of you and literally bring you to your knees. You probably wouldn't think so now seeing how easy it is to have marriages annulled or dissolved. But if you've never experienced the trauma of physically, mentally, and emotionally severing ties to someone that you were in full swing of building a life with, then I wouldn't expect you to understand. The flood of emotions that accompany the tragedy of divorce is devastating!

I consider it a tragedy because it involves death. The death of a relationship, partnership, and a love that you believed you would have forever. It also marks the death of hopes and dreams that you both shared, and for a season, the death of joy, peace, and happiness that almost seemed effortless before. I guess these emotions could vary from person to person depending on where you are in your life at the time, and what the relationship was actually like for the duration of the marriage. But, I think it's safe to assume that it couldn't have been too much of a good thing because of the end result. It is not my intent to be critical here, but rather, my attempt to state the obvious.

When my ex-husband and I decided to divorce, it was a pain that I thought I would never get over. To be honest, because we shared a lot of the same friends and acquaintances, I'm not sure if I was more concerned about the condition of my heart, or what people would think. Sometimes, we're not as affected by what happens to us as we are by our own perception of it. But, in my case, it was likely a wide combination of both.., but no less difficult either way.

When I arrived in Italy in January of 1999, my marriage was already in shambles. It was lying at death's door and I had no idea if it would survive. He had already been in Naples for ten months prior to my arrival. Although I was hopeful; the situation was critical. It would take a miracle to save it and restore it back to health. We were barely communicating at this point, and here I was flying thousands of miles to be closer to him so that we could continue our so-called life together. Or, at least as close as possible because he was stationed in one city and me another. God knew what He was doing.

I decided to put my trust in God and let Him work out the details. I committed to just putting one foot in front of the other and letting God be my guide...my strength. I really had no clue where I would find myself by the time this trial was over, but the one thing I was sure of without question or hesitation is that God was in control! He had my back, and He was going to bring me through it. Maybe not in the way that I wanted or expected, but ultimately it would be the best thing for me. It would be for my good, and for His glory.

So, to make a long story short, after seeing my husband for the first time in ten months, it was clear that what we once shared no longer existed. After two years of marriage, the relationship was over. Before I had even arrived on the Island, I believe he had already made his decision; and he had not chosen me. It was heartbreaking, it was humiliating, and it was embarrassing. I felt like a complete failure, and I got stuck in the rejection.

Now, let's be clear; I am not the least bit interested in playing the victim. He does not shoulder all the blame for the breakdown of our marriage. It was doomed from the very beginning, but I believe we shared an equal part in the failure. Where he fell short in some areas, I'm sure I fell short in others.

Although I had been saved for over a year when we married, I knew my husband wasn't saved. But we were both attending Church services regularly, and I felt pretty confident that he was leaning in that direction. I was wrong. At the end of the day, we were never meant to be life partners. We weren't equally yoked (2 Corinthians 6:14).

I never really quite understood that scripture back then, being still very young in my Christian development. But as a result of my choices, I had to learn through first-hand experience. I personally think that this is really important to consider for those who are in serious dating relationships, and are contemplating marriage. The bible clearly states, "How can two walk together unless they agree?" Agreement means if we are going to walk together in life, then we simply must be going in the same direction (Amos 3:3). We might have different views on some things, different careers, some different interests and things that we enjoy. In most cases, it's the things that are unique and different about us that draw people to us in the first place. Those are the things that make relationships thrive and grow. But, at the same time, we should share the same value and belief systems. We have to be on the same page so that when trouble comes, we'll have a strong foundation on which to stand. Anything less is a recipe for disaster, and will more than likely lead to a future paved with heartache and pain. Relationships are hard enough as it is; why add an even greater disadvantage to the equation?

For those of you who are currently married, and in a similar situation; just keep praying and being a godly example for your spouse, and let them be influenced by your behavior. There are many cases where only one spouse in the marriage is saved, but the bible tells us that *the unbelieving husband is sanctified by the wife, and the unbelieving wife is sanctified by the husband* (1 Corinthians 7:14).

In my case, although I didn't want the divorce, I didn't challenge it. I felt like God had spoken, so let the Church say "Amen." But I was broken. And in the midst of my brokenness, I made the decision to try it God's way, and I humbled myself and sat at His feet so that I could learn from him, heal and become the healthy and whole person that He created me to be. I didn't always like the things he revealed about me, about my motives and my need to be in control of everything, but I did take accountability for them.

He showed me how liberating real submission could be, and the power of surrender. It was a very humbling process, and a painful one, too.., but now I get it. I paid the price to learn the lesson because I lived it. I've learned that there will be many things, including people and relationships that we lose, and some that we just have to walk away from in order to receive what God has for us. We can't keep holding on to things that we know aren't good for us for the sake of pride. And staying in relationships just for convenience, and thinking that a wrong relationship is better than no relationship at all. There is absolutely no truth to that…at all! But what is true is that sometimes we have to make hard decisions; even if it means being alone for a season.

I want to speak to those of you who have suffered the pain and disappointment of failure in any area. And those of you who may be smack dab in the middle of it right now.., even divorce. I want you to know that this is not the end of your story. Life doesn't end just because a dream, a relationship, friendship, job, or business does. No, life gets better if you have the courage to keep living it; if you will yourself to get up and move forward.

Know that this loss is a blessing in disguise, and that God has so much more in store for you. But, He had to get you out of that situation so that you could experience His best.

He has delivered you from the thing that caused you to lower your expectations. He delivered you from the thing that was hurting you, diminishing you, and causing you to settle for less than you're worth.

Now, that in no way implies that the person you were with was a bad person. It just simply means that he or she was not the right person for you. And likewise, you were not the right person for them. God has better for both of you. He has loosed the chains that had you bound and He has set you free. Now is the time to work on you; to focus on being the best you that you can possibly be. Open yourself up to the possibilities in this season, and watch God give you beauty for ashes.

When making important decisions in our lives, we should be led by the Holy Spirit and not our flesh. We have to decide that we are no longer willing to settle for less than God's best; less than the abundant life that He has promised us. We have to be courageous enough to choose *better,* and wise enough to know what *better* is. What it looks and feels like…spiritually. That's not only applicable to our romantic relationships, but in so many other areas of our lives as well.

As long as we exist on this earth, there will be storms that impact our lives in some way, form or fashion. It may show up in the form of divorce, relationship troubles, domestic abuse, unemployment, bankruptcy, foreclosure, alcoholism, substance abuse, health challenges, problems with your children, or unrealized academic goals. The list goes on and on.

The storms' level of intensity will vary from season to season, and situation to situation, but they have no respect of persons. To put it plainly…life happens! But it's not the end of the world. President Obama said it best when he stated that, "The only end of the world is the end of the world." I agree.., and unless you die tomorrow, the sun will rise again, and the gift of a new day will come. It's totally within your power to choose what you will do with that gift. If you've ever heard the phrase, *"Each new day is a gift from God, but what we do with it is our gift to Him,"* then you understand what I mean.

The point that I want to make is this; don't get stuck in the failures of your past, and on life's issues that were only meant to strengthen your core and prepare you for your destiny. Put your big girl panties on (or your big guy briefs), and deal with it. Get past it and move on! Let your heavenly Father see you using the power that He's given you to overcome every obstacle and adversity, and walk in victory!

CHAPTER 9
No Guts, No Glory

I discovered yesterday that it's not the end of the world when you walk in late for Church on a Sunday morning and literally fall into your seat with half of the congregation… *and* the Pastor, watching. Well, while it may not be the end of the world, it sure is embarrassing! But listen, if the truth be told, I've been through much worse. In fact, if they were to do a television series on life's most embarrassing moments, I'd probably have a pretty good shot at making the show.

What I also discovered, is that the significant thing about yesterday is that…*it's in the past!* It's behind you. The world has moved on. I admit that this example is on the lighter, more humorous side of the spectrum. But the fact of the matter is that at some point, we're all going to have to deal with some challenges.

With that being said, sometimes even when you're making progress, it feels like you're losing…like nothing is working in your favor. Don't buy into that lie. Regardless of how it looks or feels in that moment, the truth is that you're really winning, and all things are working together for your good.

When I left my last job, I was just a few days shy of completing two full years. After giving it everything I had and exerting tons of energy and effort into it; I finally came to terms with the fact that no matter how hard I tried it just was not going to work out. Although being able to work independently was a benefit, the bottom line is that it wasn't a good fit for me.

My mother tried everything in her power to get me to quit for the better part of a year. But, I kept holding on thinking that things would get better. Sometimes, we have a tendency to try to hold on to things simply because we dread the thought of having to start over somewhere else. Basically, we stay for convenience, or because we seem to think that we have something to prove, and our pride won't let us leave…even when we are clearly drowning.

I'm not one to give up easily and walk away from something that I really want, or something that's important to me. If I were, you certainly wouldn't be reading this book right now. However, there comes a time when you have to discern when your time is up in any situation; whether it's a job, a relationship, or whatever the case may be. At the end of the day, you have to have the wisdom to know when it is no longer worth the energy and effort that you are putting into it.

Well, after struggling on that job for nearly two full years, I started getting that all-too-familiar feeling of restlessness. For me, that has always been a clear indicator that I'm not where I'm supposed to be, and it would soon be time for me to move on. I honestly didn't know what my next move was going to be. But, what I did know for sure was that this was not the life that I wanted to wake up to every morning for years to come. Shoot, I'm on the second half of my life…middle-aged status! And after retiring from the military and going back to school full-time to finish my degree, I felt like I had earned the right to at least be doing something that I enjoyed. So, I jumped!

I finally made the decision to leave that job, and I submitted my resignation with a full two weeks' notice. Being military, I have great respect for leadership and therefore don't subscribe to burning bridges. So, I worked every day and continued to give a hundred percent effort until my last day. And then I walked out the door, jumped in my truck, put it in gear, and never looked back!

As I was driving away, I felt free. For whatever reason God had me in that environment, I knew that the job had served its purpose. There were lessons that I needed to learn there, and tests that I had to endure in order to develop and strengthen my character. Some of which were very painful. Most importantly, I understood that it was only meant to be a temporary stop on my road to destiny; but now it was time to move on.

Decision-making is risky. But dreamers were built to take risks. I believe that some of you are dreamers…that some of you have that feeling in your gut that is telling you that there's got to be more to life than this! You feel like you're not living up to your full potential; that there is more that you were called to do. I believe that this is your time.., your moment to get out of the boat and start walking on the water. This is your season to take steps of faith towards your purpose and destiny. God is calling you out of the sidelines, and beckoning you to get up and get in the game!

It takes faith to move beyond fear; to step out of your comfort zone into the unknown. But faith without works is dead. Hebrews 11:1 states that *faith is the substance of things hoped for and the evidence of things not seen.* The scripture text actually reads, *NOW faith is…* That tells those of us who believe God to do some amazing things in our future, that *now* is the time, and this is the point in our lives to take that leap of faith. We've been thinking about it for a long time. Dreaming about it, and even talking about it to some extent, but at some point we have to stop just thinking, dreaming and talking.., and be proactive in making our dreams a reality. Any and everybody can dream, and that's a great thing. But, it's the risk takers among us who are actually willing to take that next step. To jump, even when we don't know where we will land.

I read a statement not too long ago in a Kingdom Connection Devotional by Jentezen Franklin Ministries that said, "Faith is the ability to jump and trust God, even when you can't see. It opens doors and frees us from every prison of fear." To me, that's confirmation that allowing ourselves to be vulnerable is liberating. It takes guts to put ourselves out there; to move even when we are afraid. But, guess what? No guts, no glory! No risk, no reward!

I often prayed that God would help me fulfill the dream that I believe He put in my heart of writing this book. Although I was extremely afraid of putting myself out there and exposing some of my personal struggles, I was willing to get out of my comfort zone and do it anyway.., to do it afraid, and trust Him for the outcome., *and they overcame him by the blood of the Lamb, and by the word of their testimony* (Revelations 12:11). After all, if you're not willing to share what you've been through, then what's the purpose of going through?

All I needed was an opportunity where I had the time and the resources to commit to getting it done. For years, I would always start and stop, start and stop, start and stop. I had a hard time staying focused because of other things that demanded my attention. When I was working, I was always too physically and mentally drained to sit and concentrate on my writing after work. So, once again, the book got put on the back burner. I didn't see how it would ever be possible under my current circumstances. There just didn't seem to be enough time in the day. Honestly, I was starting to give up on the whole idea. But God said, "Not so!"

The next thing I knew, I was putting in my resignation...and now, here we are just a little over a year later, and you're reading this book. Now it all makes sense. There was a reason why I felt restless at my job, and why it just didn't work out, no matter how hard I tried. God had something better in mind. If I was willing to step out on faith and try, then He was more than willing to make a way for me to get it done. Won't He do it?!!

It's not that He did anything miraculous to make it happen in this situation with my job. Obviously, I was in a position where I was able to walk away from it and be okay financially for a season. But, what He did was make it difficult for me to stay in a situation where if I *had* prospered, I would have become content to just stay there and earn a pay check. And, I would probably never have reached for anything higher. I would have *settled* for less than what God has in store for me. Sometimes, God has to close doors when it's time for us to move forward because He knows that we won't move unless we are forced to by our circumstances.

I want to encourage someone who is reading this book right now.., someone who may be feeling restless in your current situation. Whatever is in your heart to do, even if you're afraid- do it afraid! Just take a step. Allow yourself the freedom of being vulnerable. That's how you find out what you're really made of. I'd be willing to bet you'd discover that you're stronger than you think. Don't be afraid to make some tough decisions, even when you're not totally sure you're doing the right thing. Yes, you'll likely make some mistakes along the way but, such is life. The vast majority of us get it wrong sometimes. Probably more often than we get it right.

Have the faith to believe that *in all things we are more than conquerors; we are overcomers through Christ Jesus* (Romans 8:37). Don't get stuck in the failures and shame of your past. Yesterday is over and done. Today is a brand new day. Let's make it count!

CHAPTER 10
God is a Promise Keeper

    I want to share a very special experience that I had with God several years ago that will hopefully bless somebody the way that it still blesses me every time I think about it. It was during a very trying time in my life when I was feeling down, depressed, disappointed and discouraged. I had believed God for some very specific blessings to take place during this particular year, and things just were not working out. Many of the Pastors and Bishops on the popular TV ministries that I tuned in to faithfully were all preaching about finishing strong as we approached the end of the year and were preparing to bring in the next one with faith, hope, anticipation, and great expectation.

    I was pretty excited and motivated for the majority of the year, just knowing that God was going to move on my behalf and give me at least some of what I asked for. Maybe I was going to finally meet the man that I had been *somewhat* patiently waiting for, or maybe this was the year that I was going to get the promotion on my job that I earnestly prayed for. I can't even remember now all of the things that I had asked and believed God for, but I assure you they all seemed important at the time. And I was expecting Him to move on at least a couple of them before the end of the year, you know.., so I could *finish strong*.

Well, I'm sure you have figured out by now that things didn't exactly go as planned. The year quickly progressed as months gave way to weeks, and weeks gave way to days, and the days gave way to just hours that ultimately brought what seemed like an uneventful year to an end. Promotion season came and went, and my name didn't magically appear on the list. The months began to fly by, and still that perfect man was nowhere to be found. Now, don't get me wrong; there was an abundance of men out there who were available to date and who could've probably filled the time and space in the places where I was experiencing a void. But, the challenge for me was in meeting the *right* man, or at least the right man for me. I'm not talking about perfection. We all know by now that there simply are no perfect people who walk this earth. We all come with our own personal set of flaws, shortcomings, and insecurities. I think the key is in knowing and understanding yourself so that you will know the type of person that will compliment you, and help balance you out. I just don't believe in wasting time (theirs or mine), getting to know someone on that level who I already know isn't going to be a good fit for me.

In any case, I remember on this particular day, I was on my way to Ahoskie, NC to get my car inspected since I lived in Virginia but still had NC tags on the car. I remember feeling heavy and depressed. I felt like the end of the year had come and none of the things God had promised me had come to pass. I was terribly disappointed to say the least, and I was in no mood to talk to anybody or do anything other than have my own little pity party…, right then, and right there!

When I finally arrived at the service station to get the inspection, I was told that the wait was 30 minutes. No problem there, I had nowhere else to be. I was sad and feeling sorry for myself, so it didn't matter to me if it took them all of that day and part of the next. I just wanted somewhere to sit down and quickly return to the pitiful little party I was throwing myself where I was the only person in attendance. The one I was having in my spirit where no one else was welcome unless they were feeling the exact same way that I was. No room for happy people. They just simply would not be tolerated…, not today! I mean, after all.., it was my party and I could cry if I wanted to…right?

So, as I sat in my car waiting to be served, I decided to have a little talk with Jesus, you know.., and tell him all about my troubles. I was honest with God, and I told him how I was feeling. Of course He already knew because He knows me better than I know myself.

I have found through my walk with God over the years that if we have even a whisper of what could possibly qualify as a personal relationship with God, we can learn to discern what He is trying to do in us and through us. Maybe not immediately…, it may take some time for our spiritual eyes to come open and fully focus, but eventually we should be able to see the truth in every situation. So I proceeded to talk with God and I let him know that I was disappointed that He had not done what he said he was going to do in my life during that year. The year was pretty much over and done, and I had not finished strong. Not unless He was going to do it in the next 24 to 48 hours. And even though I knew He could do it if he chose to, it just was not likely to happen for me this year, period.

As the 30 minutes quickly flew by, and my car was next in line to be inspected, I was directed to an inside lounge where I could comfortably wait in the company of a few other customers and a 32" tv. The other option was a cute little bench right outside the station where I could enjoy the peace and quiet and fresh air, and be alone with my thoughts once again. I chose the latter. It was pretty warm outside at the time. Unseasonably warm as a matter of fact, for the end of December in North Carolina. So, as I nonchalantly took my seat on the bench, I was determined to return to the conversation I was having with God. Before I could even focus my thoughts to pick up where I left off, I just happened to look up at a billboard that was positioned right across the street from me in my direct view. Written on that billboard was the most timely, powerful message I could have received at that moment. In large bold letters the billboard simply read, *GOD Is a Promise Keeper!* I could feel my eyes welling up with tears as the weight of the discouragement and disappointment lifted off of me, and as I relaxed in the peace that God gave me at that moment.

It was confirmation that God had heard my heart's cry, and He was very aware of the burden of disappointment and discouragement that I was carrying at that moment. This personalized intimate moment with God was to let me know that those promises were still good, but they would be fulfilled according to His timing, not mine. I had no choice but to confront the fact that I had imposed those time constraints. He never said that those things would happen that year. That was all me being a little over zealous in my faith.

Now let's be clear, there is absolutely nothing wrong with believing God for a specific blessing or miracle to come to pass at a specific time. We know that God responds to faith. The bible says that *without faith it is impossible to please God* (Hebrews 11:6). I am also reminded of a certain scripture in the bible where Jesus says, *"Blessed is she that believed, for there shall be a performance of those things promised to her."* (Luke 1:45).

God is pleased with our willingness to step out on faith, and dare to believe Him to move on our behalf in any situation, especially one that we have earnestly prayed over. I believe faith will get God's attention quicker than anything else will. But, in the midst of all the praying and believing, declaring and decreeing, we have to remember to humble ourselves enough to say, "Nevertheless, not my will, but thine be done," Amen. (Luke 22:42)

That means no matter what God decides to do in our situation, it's perfectly ok. It means that if He does or even if He doesn't, I'm still going to serve Him. I'm still going to love Him with all of my mind, my heart, and my strength. I'm still going to endeavor to be the best me that I know how to be, and I'm still going to give God the glory in all things and for all things. He's still worthy. He's still God! That's a sign of growth and spiritual maturity. That, in a manner of speaking is putting away childish things (1 Corinthians 13:11).

There comes a time when we have to realize that what we want isn't always the best thing for us. God knows what's best for us in every situation and circumstance, and God never fails. He's never late. He's always on time. He may not move in the way we want him to, but He moves in the way that he knows is best for us. He always has our best interest at heart.

So, as I paid the mechanic, hopped in my jeep and started on the hour-long trip back home, I was amazed to notice the difference those few moments alone with God made in my life. I definitely did not leave the same way I came. I left encouraged, revived, full of joy, and inspired to keep moving forward.

My spirit was at peace, and I felt like I had the strength to go a little bit further on this journey. Nope, there would be no giving up for this ol' girl. Not that day! On a cloudy day in December several years ago, out of all the people walking the face of this earth, God looked down and saw me. At that moment He looked beyond my faults and saw my need.

As it turns out, God was faithful to promote me to Chief Petty Officer…in His timing. He did it when he knew I was ready to handle the blessing. He blessed me to complete 22 years of active military service, retire and go back to school fulltime to complete my Bachelor's Degree at Virginia Wesleyan University. Now, I'm a published Author, and I'm learning new things about myself every day. I love my life! And I'm excited about my future…about what's next.

Will I ever get married again? I don't know. Only God has the answer to that question. While I'm open to the possibilities.., it's certainly not a requirement for me to be happy. I'm already there! I'm living a full life, doing the things that I've always wanted to do, meeting new people, forming new relationships (personal and professional), and pushing myself so far out of my comfort zone that it's beyond scary…it's exhilarating! In fact, when it comes to marriage, I kind of feel like I've been there, done that- so I'm not pressed. But, if it's meant to be, I believe that He will bring the right guy into my life at the appointed time. Someone who will be able to relate to my experience and can appreciate what I bring to the relationship…and vice-versa.

    Trust me…my story is far from over. I'm still in the middle of it. He's still writing it, and I'm still walking it out… one step and one day at a time.

CHAPTER 11
Who I'm Becoming

 Do you ever look in the mirror and notice that you're not the same person that you were a year ago, a month ago, or even a few days ago? I do. I don't mean it in the physical sense. I'm speaking of the person that you are *becoming*...spiritually, intellectually, and psychologically. I'm talking about growth and change as a whole person. I recognize as time goes by and with different situations that I encounter, that I am changing. And I love it!

 Change is good. If you are evolving and growing as a person, then there is no way that you can still be the same person that you were last year. You should be learning new things, visiting new places, experiencing foods you've never tasted before, and meeting new people. You should also be dreaming new dreams, and challenging yourself to grow and stretch and achieve more than you ever imagined you could. In essence, you should be changing for the better, and loving who you are becoming. With these positive changes, we become stronger, more vibrant and confident people.

 When we are trying to grow, we make changes that add value to our lives, and positively influence the lives of others. Even if we are not where we think we should be, we feel confident that we are moving in the right direction. The fact of the matter is that we're not in the same place that we were last year. That's progress. That's forward motion.

This is so relevant to me right now because of my past failures and struggles. The times in my life when I didn't feel so good about who I was. I guess you can call it low self-esteem because I let other people's opinion of me affect how I saw myself. I struggled to understand and really believe that I was who God said that I was. I wanted to be accepted just like everybody else. I wanted to *fit in* just like everybody else seemed to.

I didn't know that I was being rejected because God was shining His light on me the whole time. I didn't realize then that *friendship with the world meant enmity with God* (James 4:4). That I wasn't meant to fit in, and that God was calling me to stand out and be different. Not any better or less than anyone else…just different. He was grooming and challenging me to be courageous enough to chart my own path; to be true to who I really am and not who people want me to be.

God wanted me to be strong, courageous, and sure of myself in Him. It took me a while to really get it.., to really understand what He was birthing in me. The truth is, I'm still learning. The process was and still is excruciatingly painful at times. I say that because you never really arrive. It's never over as long as you still have breath in your body and the blood is still running warm in your veins.

Destiny doesn't stop and neither does purpose. Once you conquer and achieve one goal, then you have to be ready to move on to the next. You have to be ever learning and seeking new knowledge, and putting what you've learned into action. Otherwise you stop growing and evolving, and you become stagnant, irrelevant and ineffective.

Now that I've somewhat figured it out, and have chosen (in humble submission) to go through the process as the Lord leads, I love what it is awakening in me. I love the person that I see. What I have always known about myself but, in recent years have developed an even deeper awareness of is the fact that I have somewhat of a quiet strength that rises to the surface whenever I need it the most. The bible describes it as having a meek spirit. The problem with that is that people sometimes mistake meekness for weakness. They fail to understand that meekness is really strength under control. It means that no matter how hard you try to bully, humiliate or provoke me, if I can help it, I'm not going to let you cause me to act outside of my character. That means, I'm not going to let you bring me down to your level; you're going to have to come up to mine. This is especially true with people who are so miserable in their own lives that when they see you shining and *flossing* (slang), they make it their mission in life to try to bring you down. They are called bullies. At the end of the day, all bullies really want from you is a reaction, and if you neglect to give them that, they lose. They lose in more ways than one. They lose power, they lose an audience, they lose influence, they lose credibility, and eventually they lose interest.

I know from first-hand experience that it can be really difficult to deal with, especially in the workplace when it's hidden under the guise of passive aggressive-type bullying that can be very subtle and hard to prove. Choose your battles wisely. Fight only the things that are truly worth your time and effort, otherwise…let it roll off of you like water off of a duck's back. Keep smiling, and keep moving forward. These are just minor road bumps on your way to destiny.

Today, it gives me great pleasure to say that even as I'm writing this book, I'm feeling strong, and confident, and I love it! I love the changes that I'm seeing in me. I know that after all I have been through, that I can stand on my own two feet because I've had to. Didn't expect or want anybody to *give* me anything. Everything that I have, I paid a price for it. Every promotion I've ever received, I earned it and God found me faithful.

I know today that I can properly filter and process the pain of failure and brokenness because I've been tested in those areas over and over again. I can handle rejection because I've experienced rejection and being ostracized many times over. I don't feel the need to be validated; at least not by the world. The world can't be trusted. The only opinion that matters is God's…and His word tells us that we are fearfully and wonderfully made (Psalm 139:14). Everything that God created was good and very good. That includes you and me.

When it's all said and done, I have to know who I am for myself, regardless of what others think. I have to be strong enough in my convictions to hold my head up high and stand on that thing!

So, now that we've come to the place of self-acceptance and loving the person that we are becoming, it's time to stop hiding. Come out of the shadows and let your light shine.

It's time to take some risks in life, and try some new things. It's time to open up and let the world in. It's time to let people know who you really are…the *real you*, whether they accept you or not. If they don't accept you, then they are not meant to be a part of your story. And even if it's extremely scary…it's time to be vulnerable, and transparent. You've got nothing at all to lose, but everything to gain.

Believe in the inner-most, depths of your being that you can survive the storms of life if you just keep moving, living, evolving and becoming. I know its cliché, but as the saying goes, *everything that doesn't kill you only makes you stronger.* You have to believe that you have the power to overcome. You can't let the issues of life stop you. You can't let failure and disappointments kill your dreams. You must overcome! (Revelation 2:26). Trust your instincts, step out on faith, and keep moving forward. I'm ready, are you?

CHAPTER 12
This Far by Faith

    I would venture to say that some of you reading this book right now, before you got sidetracked by whatever obstacle or trial you are currently facing, you were on your way somewhere. Well, the word for you today is, *"Get back on course, and move forward."* No more going nowhere fast. Purpose awaits you, and destiny is calling! This is the day to get back on the path to greatness. God has amazing things in store for you, and I personally can't wait for the unveiling.

    If you are anything like me, many of you probably feel like it's been a long time coming. But, guess what? The time has finally arrived, and this is your season! God is moving in your situation, and working all things together for your good. Whatever you go through now or in the future, if it causes you to pray and lean on Jesus more than you have in the past…*then it's working for you a far more exceeding and eternal weight of glory* (2 Corinthians 4:17). Just know that the trying of your faith produces tremendous power in your life and in your relationship with God. Knowing that God is in control should be the very thing that ultimately gives us comfort, and the courage to trust Him in the midst of our struggles. It gives us the assurance that no matter what the enemy tries to do to stop us; *no weapon formed against us will prosper* (Isaiah 54:17). If God be for us, He is more than the whole world against us.

Whatever you are believing God for in this season, if it is part of his perfect plan for your life, trust Him to bring it to pass in His timing. Have the faith to believe that if God has called you to do it, then He will get you to it and through it, successfully. Your part is to pray, stand firm in your faith, and work hard. Be open to hear and receive direction from God so that you will know the way in which He is leading you, and so that you will be successful in all you do.

Now, nobody ever said that it was going to be easy. Trust and believe that there will be some battles to be fought along the way. But, the bible tells us that the devil is defeated and that we have the victory in Christ Jesus.

When I finally said yes to God, and made the decision to move forward with writing and publishing this book, I did so because I didn't want to go through the rest of my life wondering, *what if?* I had to fight through distractions, insecurities, fear, and many other obstacles that the enemy used to oppose me; and was often left feeling discouraged and defeated. I could've let those things stop me, but I knew that if I did, it would mean that I was still living a defeated life.

Well, I don't know about you, but I've already given fear too much of my past. I refuse to let that continue to be my story. I'm moving forward! And I'm trusting God to lead the way.., *to be a lamp unto my feet, and a light unto my pathway* (Psalm 119:105).

It's true that we all come with our own set of gifts, talents, and abilities.., some of which many of us have yet to tap into. I'm praying that God will continue to stir up the gifts that are lying dormant inside of me, and cause me reach, and live up to my full potential in Him. I pray that over your life as well. After all, who really knows in what capacity God is going to use any of us?

What I do know is this…I'm available, and I'm willing to be used in any capacity that He chooses. When it's all said and done, I want to know that my life was useful for something more than just getting up in the morning and going to bed at night. I want to know that I did some very meaningful things in between.

I don't want to look back over my life with regret. I want to know that I took some risks, and tried some things…even if I fail. At least I know I tried. I didn't just sit on the side lines and watch everybody else live out their dreams while I was too fearful to pursue my own.

I firmly believe that God has given us unlimited opportunities to do great things, and it's our duty to take advantage of it while we still have the chance. He said that He would make our name great, and I believe him. Not for us to be boastful or for our own selfish ambition.., but so that we can leave a legacy behind for those generations that will come after us.

While traveling on this road to destiny, one of the most impactful things that I've learned along the way is that life gets better as you give yourself permission to live it. Living it means getting out of your comfort zone, and doing the things that you've always wanted to do, but were just too afraid to try.

If I could give some meaningful advice to a receiving heart right now, I would say, "Be vulnerable! Take a chance at something. And regardless of the setbacks, the opposition, the failures and the disappointments.., get up from where you are and move forward! You've come this far by faith- you might as well go all the way!"

Today, make the decision to get out of the boat, step out on faith and chase after your dreams…your destiny. Destiny can't stop here…God has more for you to do!

Every now and again I take a moment to reflect back over the carefree years of my life when I left home at 18 years old and joined the Navy. I left my friends, my family, my boyfriend at the time, my pets, my car, and everything that was familiar and comfortable to me. I didn't know it then, but that took faith and courage, especially for the timidly shy and somewhat naïve kid that I was back then.

Who knew then that God was about to take me on an amazing journey? There would be many ups and downs, peaks and valleys, successes and failures, victories and defeats. But after it was all said and done, God would cause me to triumph and bring me out stronger and wiser than I've ever been. As I look back at where I started from to where I now stand; and as I endeavor to keep moving forward in faith, I say to myself, "What a journey, but no regrets. The best is yet to come!"

Amen, somebody!

THE JOURNEY
Forward

Sometimes, the way up is down
On bended knee in prayer from the heart.
Sometimes, the way forward is back
Back to that old landmark.
Return, O' return to your first love
Take a step forward in faith.
Tired of being stagnant in my growth
There's got to be a better way.

Yesterday's sorrows I've left behind
To be remembered no more.
No more living in the past
The future has much in store.
Made up my mind to get up from here
And do it without delay.
My faith is leading me to move forward
And Jesus is the way.

I will not fear the journey ahead
No matter where it leads.
I won't forego the process

No matter what it brings.
My heart is fixed, my mind's made up
I will not compromise.
And though the enemy knocks me down
My faith says, *still I rise!*

It ain't over, it ain't done
The battle yet reigns on.
I will not stop, I will not quit
Until the victory is won!
Forward in faith is where I'm headed
Destiny is the goal.
The journey forward can't stop here
There are miles and miles to go!

Prayer

Father God, I pray over the life of every person that will come in contact with this book. I pray that You would give us the strength to overcome every obstacle that the enemy puts in our way, and the courage to run after our dreams with passion. I acknowledge that You are a loving and sincere God that cares deeply about your people. I pray that You would shine your light on us as we seek You for forward direction in our lives, and believe in faith that every necessary provision will be made on our behalf. Mend us, heal us and restore us to the whole person that You created us to be; fully dependent on You and your power to heal, deliver and set us free. Restore unto us the joy of your salvation. Empower each of us to be strong and influential servants of faith as we move forward on this journey. We are forever mindful to give You all of the honor, the glory and the praise.

-*Amen.*

QUESTIONS

1. In what areas of your life have you allowed failures and setbacks to keep you from moving forward with your dreams?

2. Reflect on a scripture that has been particularly impactful in your life during seasons of struggle.

3   What are some scriptures that can help you overcome fear and walk in the power of God?

4   In the Bible, what are some of the things that God teaches us about faith?

5   In what ways can the negative effects of rejection be turned into a positive in your life?

6   Think about possible areas in your life where you may be harboring unforgiveness and resentment towards others, and ask God to help you release the debt, and forgive the offense.

7   In what ways can you use the power of your testimony to witness to others, and encourage them to keep moving forward?

8   What does the term *Forward in Faith* mean to you?

9   In what ways has God called you to move forward in your life?

10 What major thing would you attempt to accomplish if fear was not an issue?

11 Starting today, in what way can you take steps toward fulfilling your destiny?

Journal

As you read this book, I encourage you to use the following pages to reflect on your own journey, and write down your thoughts, experiences, road blocks, and possible ways to move forward. Then, after you have begun to make progress, come back, review the journal, measure your progress, and see just how far you have moved *Forward in Faith*.

CHAPTER 1 *It's a Process*

CHAPTER 2 *This Too Shall Pass*

CHAPTER 3 *Challenge Your Fears*

CHAPTER 4 *Handling Rejection*

CHAPTER 5 *The Truth*

CHAPTER 6 *Unforgiveness*

CHAPTER 7 *Purpose in Brokeness*

CHAPTER 8 *Forward After Failure*

CHAPTER 9 *No Guts, No Glory*

CHAPTER 10 — *God is a Promise Keeper*

CHAPTER 11 *Who I'm Becoming*

CHAPTER 12 *This Far by Faith*

Made in the USA
Middletown, DE
16 July 2017